**Houghton
Mifflin
Harcourt**

READING Adventures

Welcome, Reader!

In this magazine you will discover that creepy things can be cool—especially spiders, frogs, turtles, and pythons. You'll learn how John Muir helped to create Yosemite National Park and how kids like you help to protect their own local habitats.

You'll read poems and articles about museums and nature, and explore even more in lots of fun activities.

Your path to discovery begins when you turn the page!

"Spider Ropes" from *A Nest Full of Stars* by James Berry. Text copyright © 2002 by James Berry. Reprinted by permission of HarperCollins Publishers. "The Spider" by Jack Prelutsky from *Something Big Has Been Here*. Copyright © 1990 by Jack Prelutsky. Reprinted by permission of HarperCollins Publishers. "The Poison-Dart Frogs" from *Lizards, Frogs, and Polliwogs* by Douglas Florian. Copyright © 2001 by Douglas Florian. Reprinted by permission of Houghton Mifflin Harcourt Publishing Company. "Toad by the Road" from *Toad by the Road: A Year in the Life of These Amazing Amphibians* by Joanne Ryder. Text copyright © 2007 by Joanne Ryder. Reprinted by permission of Henry Holt and Company, LLC. "Museum Farewell" by Rebecca Kai Dotlich. Text copyright © 2007 by Rebecca Kai Dotlich. Reprinted by permission of Curtis Brown Ltd. "The Comb of Trees" by Claudia Lewis from *Up In the Mountains: And Other Poems of Long Ago*. Text copyright © 1991 by Claudia Lewis. Reprinted by permission of HarperCollins Publishers. "Naming the Turtle" by Patricia Hubbell from *The Tigers Brought Pink Lemonade*. Text copyright © 1988 by Patricia Hubbell. Reprinted by permission of the author c/o Marian Reiner, Literary Agent. "Greater Flamingo" from *An Old Shell: Poems of the Galapagos* by Tony Johnston. Text copyright © 1999 by Tony Johnston. Reprinted by permission of Farrar, Straus & Giroux LLC. "Dinosaur Bone" from *Keepers* by Alice Schertle. Copyright © 1996 by Alice Schertle. Reprinted by permission of the author, who controls all rights.

2014 Edition
Copyright © 2014 by Houghton Mifflin Harcourt Publishing Company

Printed in the U.S.A.

ISBN: 978-0-547-86582-9

16 17 18 19-0928-21 20 19 18 17 16 15   4500534602

Unit 6

The Girl Who Loved Spiders

I hate spiders. That's the first thing you should know about me.

My mom and I just moved from New York to Florida. That's the second thing you should know about me. We moved because my mom got a new teaching job at a university here.

Before we moved, my best friend, Billy, told me all kinds of creepy stories about spiders that live in Florida.

"My brother knows a guy from there who got bitten by a brown recluse spider," Billy said. "This guy was *smart* about spiders, too. He shook out his shoes. He watched his step. His bite healed, but it was the *worst*."

Mom has told me it takes three weeks to make a habit. It's only been a week since we moved, but I've already made one.

First thing every morning, I shake out my sneakers. Second thing, I put on my sneakers, though I'm still wearing pajamas. Third thing, I always watch my step.

Hey! Not one, but *three* new habits.

I blame them all on Billy.

I find Mom in the kitchen, drinking a glass of orange juice.

"You're awake, Luis? It's the crack of dawn!"

"Too hot."

Mom laughs. "It's summer. Aren't those winter pajamas?"

I don't tell her that flannel is better protection from spiders.

Over breakfast, Mom discusses her plan for the day. It's the same as yesterday's: unpack and settle in.

"Oh!" Mom sits up straight in her chair. "I found a dead scorpion yesterday. It was in perfect shape—not a leg missing. Fascinating, really. I saved it in case you wanted to see."

I gulp. "No thanks."

Great. Venomous spiders *and* scorpions.

Mom shrugs. "Okay. So what are you up to?"

"TV?"

Mom frowns.

"There's always the trampoline," I mutter.

Mom bought the trampoline the day after we arrived. It's as big and bouncy as can be—something I always wanted that Billy had. I just wish Billy were here now to teach me how to do a flip.

Not even 8:30 in the morning, and I'm on the trampoline again. Every jump takes me higher and higher.

In mid-air, I see her—two yards over—a girl about my age. I keep jumping. The girl kneels before a bush, in tall grass where all kinds of biting and stinging things might be. She stays very still.

Next jump, I see something in her hands . . . a pink ball?

Jump higher!

The girl claps the ball. Poof! A white cloud explodes from between her fingers.

I collapse onto the trampoline and scramble down. This I have to see. As I enter her yard, where the grass is taller, I freeze.

The ball in the girl's hands is a rolled-up sock. A camera dangles from a strap around her neck. She carefully settles the sock on the grass. Then she raises the camera and peers through it. I look where she's looking, at a delicate shape against the bush's leaves, like lace against green velvet.

The shape is a gigantic spider web, whitened by whatever the girl clapped from the sock.

Photographers sometimes make spider webs more visible by dusting them with cornstarch.

Not all spiders make their homes in webs. Some dig burrows.

"Yikes!" I yell at the sight of the web.

The girl cries out, surprised, and falls into the web. She springs up, web clinging to her. "What's the big idea?" she shouts.

"Um . . . I was warning you! Guess you don't know about brown recluse spiders?"

"Of course I do. I've been trying to find one. They're shy, like most arachnids. I've found rarer breeds, even the burrowing wolf spider. Still haven't tracked down a brown recluse." She points at the bush. "That was a common orb weaver. I've been watching her for days, until she got her web just right." The girl glares. "It sure was pretty—until you came along. Who are you, anyway?"

"Luis. I just moved here."

"My name is Ashanti. Welcome to the neighborhood." She still sounds mad.

I cross my arms over my chest. "So you're on a spider safari. Why?"

"This summer my goal is to photograph one hundred spiders. I've always loved folktales about Anansi, a true spider-man. Spiders are cool."

I don't think before I say, "No, they aren't. Spiders are disgusting."

At that, Ashanti stalks away.

That afternoon Mom drives me to a park. "Never mind the heat," she says. "There'll be boys your age."

There's a decent playground, but a sign reads: BEWARE OF SNAKES! Where there are snakes, there must be spiders. Ashanti would be in heaven. As for me . . .

There are no boys my age. Two little girls sweat it out on the slide. Mom wilts on a bench. We drive home.

As we turn onto our street, we see Ashanti crouching by a flower pot in her front yard. A woman kneels beside her.

To my horror, Mom stops the car and gets out. Mom and Mrs. Smith,

Ashanti's mom, hit it off. Mrs. Smith teaches at the university, too. Mr. Smith works for the alumni office. Ashanti and I might be in the same fifth-grade class!

"Ashanti just found her first colorful crab spider," Mrs. Smith says. "It's the fiftieth spider she's photographed for her collection."

Mom and Mrs. Smith keep talking. Ashanti photographs her spider. I trace circles in the dirt. Then Mrs. Smith asks Mom and me over for dinner. Mom agrees.

Yippee.

Ashanti rolls her eyes. She's not exactly thrilled, either.

Many crab spiders use camouflage to catch prey.

At six o'clock we're standing on the Smiths' front porch. Ashanti opens the door, and soon we sit down to dinner. The Smiths and Mom talk and laugh; Ashanti and I dig into our lasagna. Soon my plate is empty; so is Ashanti's.

She gives me a cautious look. "Want to see Anansi?" she asks quietly, so as not to interrupt the grownups.

I shrug. "I guess."

Ashanti smiles a little. "Come on."

We go into the family room. African artifacts cover three of the walls: masks, instruments, weavings, and paintings. A large bulletin board hangs on the fourth wall. About fifty photographs of spiders are mounted there. I take a deep breath and go over to the board.

I've got to admit, some of the spiders look pretty cool.

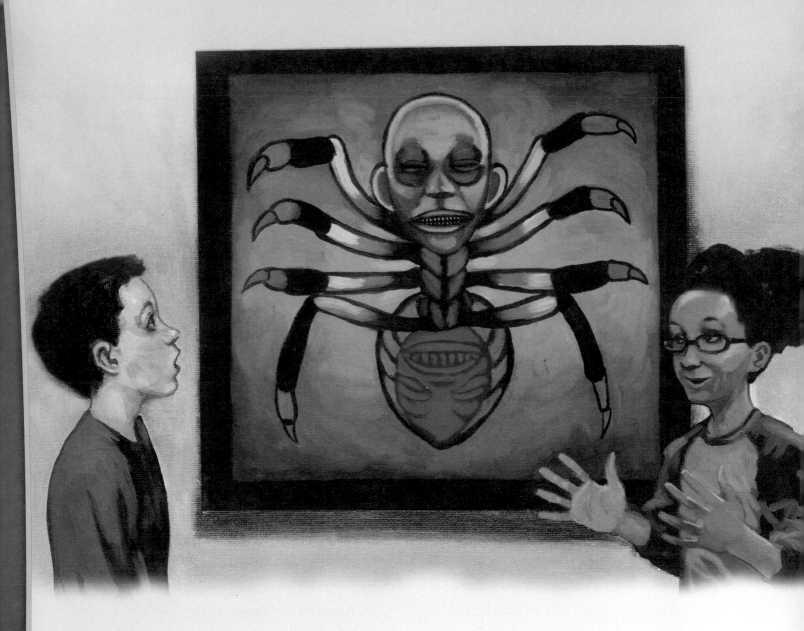

Ashanti points at a painting and says, "That's Anansi." I move closer to see a powerful-looking spider, standing upright, flexing six of its eight legs. The spider has a man's face . . . and eight eyes.

"Some legends say that Anansi created the sun, stars, and moon. Nice guy, huh?" Ashanti smiles. "He also could be tricky and greedy. In one story, he tries to keep all wisdom for himself."

Suddenly, Mrs. Smith calls from the kitchen, "Ashanti! Quick! You've got to see this!"

Ashanti turns and runs from the room with me at her heels.

Mr. and Mrs. Smith are peering at a baseboard. Ashanti presses close.

"Brown recluse!" Mrs. Smith whispers.

Ashanti gasps in excitement. She grabs her camera and adjusts the settings. Mom holds me back, although Mrs. Smith reassures her that the spider won't hurt you if you don't hurt the spider. Just don't brush up against it.

"Ashanti knows what to do, Mom," I say.

Ashanti glances at me, surprised, and smiles. Then she adjusts the zoom on her camera and snaps the picture. "Fifty-one!" she exclaims.

Later, after Mr. Smith has caught the venomous spider on a glue trap, Ashanti tells me that there's an interesting-looking web woven through my trampoline's net.

"I spotted it today on one of my safaris," she says, grinning. "I want to photograph it."

"Stop by tomorrow, if you want," I say.

"It'll be early in the morning. That's the best time."

"I'll probably be awake."

"Just don't be bouncing, OK? You might wreck it."

"I don't want to do that," I say. "I want to know which spiders live in *my* yard."

Boy, won't Billy be surprised. I'll be able to teach him a thing or two about spiders when he comes to visit!

The brown recluse spider has six eyes.

WEB WISE

Part of what makes spiders fascinating is that they weave amazing webs. Here are a few facts to make you web wise.

Web Shots

Although it can be difficult to photograph a spider web, scientists and photographers know a few tricks to make it easier.

Some use cornstarch. The white powder coats the strands of the web and makes them easier to see. However, scientists know that this can sometimes damage the web. They always remove the spider before dusting the web.

Another method doesn't harm the web at all. Photographers spray a mist of water onto a web. Drops of water cling to the web's strands. Then sunshine turns an ordinary web into a sparkling jewel!

A Sticky Situation

Have you ever wondered why spiders don't get stuck in their own webs? The answer is simple: They know where they're going.

Most webs are made from two kinds of silk. An orb spider's web, for example, has long, straight strands that start at the middle and go out to the edges, like the spokes of a wheel. Then the web has a network of spiral strands in the center. The spiral strands are sticky, but the straight strands are not.

When an insect flies or crawls into the web, it gets stuck in the sticky strands. Then the spider hurries across the long, straight strands to enjoy its next meal!

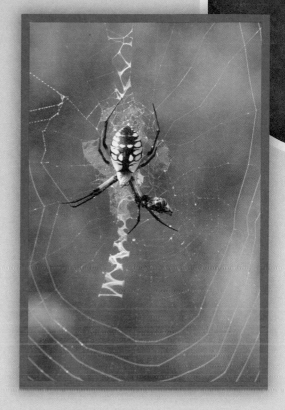

An orb spider's web is made of straight strands and spiral strands. The spiral strands are sticky.

Strange, but True!

More than 3,000 people visited a Texas state park during the 2007 Labor Day weekend. They didn't come to see parades or listen to speeches. They came to see a spider web!

It was no ordinary sight. The enormous web was draped over trees and shrubs along nearly 600 feet of a nature trail!

Scientists think millions of baby spiders, called *spiderlings*, built the web. The spiderlings may all have floated in on an air current and landed in the same area.

A few days later, heavy rain ruined the web.

The Spider

by Jack Prelutsky

The spider, sly and talented,
weaves silver webs of silken thread,
then waits for unobservant flies
... to whom she'll not apologize!

Spider Ropes

by James Berry

Alone in woods, I hunt
for pretty leaves dropped
and smooth stones like marbles.

I come back feeling
my face is well laced
with leaves and spiders' webs.

Design a Web!

If you were a spider, what kind of web would you weave? Look at the spider webs shown on this page, and then create your own design for a spider web.

Where would you make your web? What kinds of food would you hope to catch?

Write two or more sentences explaining how your web design would help you catch your lunch.

Story Scramble

Stories have a structure with a beginning, middle, and end. Events happen in an order that makes sense.

The story events below are scrambled. Put the letters in order so that the story makes sense. Then discuss how each event influences what happens next.

A. Despite the advice, Anansi threw down the pot, shouting, "The pot of wisdom is mine! I should know more than you!"

B. Anansi the spider had all the world's wisdom stored in a pot. The sky god Nyame had given it to him and told him to share it.

C. The pot broke. People found bits of wisdom scattered everywhere and took them home. That is why no one person today has all of the world's wisdom.

D. Greedy Anansi decided to hide the pot of wisdom at the top of a tree. Balancing the pot at the same time was tricky, though.

E. Anansi's young son told Anansi it would be easier to climb the tree with the pot tied to his back.

Two Tricksters
Compare and contrast Anansi's actions with those of Coyote in "The Sticky Coyote," Lesson 17, Student Book page 442.

Answers: B, D, E, A, C

17

Cool or

In "The Girl Who Loved Spiders," Luis thinks spiders are creepy until he meets Ashanti. Then he discovers that spiders are cool. Think about an animal that you really like or dislike. What is it about the animal that makes you feel the way you do? What details about the animal come to mind?

Write a poem about the animal you chose, or about an animal shown on these pages. Your poem may rhyme or use rhythm, like the poems on pages 14 and 15.

Creepy?

Use descriptive details that create a vivid picture.

Think about the following:

- the animal's appearance
- the animal's movements
- how the animal sounds
- how the animal feels to the touch

The Frog in the Milk Pail

"I'm tired of sitting on this log," croaked a frog one sunny morning. So he jumped out of his pond and hopped off to explore.

Before long, the frog reached a fence. "How curious," he said. "I wonder if it tastes good." He flicked out his long tongue.

"Ugh!" he said.

The frog hopped along until he reached a brick path. "How curious," he said. "I wonder if it tastes good." He flicked out his long tongue.

"Ick!" he said.

The frog kept hopping until he saw a barn. "How curious," he said as he hopped up to the door. Just then he heard a loud *BZZZZ*.

"It's a fly!" cried the frog. "And after all this hopping, I'm hungry. "

The frog squeezed under the barn door. A big, fat fly was flying overhead. "Yum!" said the frog as he leaped into the air, but the fly was fast and flew away.

The frog, though, didn't land where he expected to. "How curious," said the frog. "I've landed in a pond with white water and shiny silver banks." Of course, it wasn't really a pond. It was a metal pail half-full of fresh milk.

The frog tried to climb out of the pail. But he just kept sliding back into the milk. He swam and splashed and kicked. He went faster and faster.

Then the frog noticed yellow globs floating in the milk. "How curious," he said. He went on swimming and splashing and kicking. He saw more yellow globs.

Before long there was a yellow hill in the middle of the pail. All that kicking and splashing and swimming had churned the milk into butter!

The frog climbed up the butter hill and jumped out of the pail. He hopped all the way home.

The moral of the story: Never give up.

The Science of Butter

Is making butter a chemical or a physical change? In a chemical change, a new chemical substance forms. Making butter is a physical change. The chemical makeup of the milk doesn't change. Churning simply makes drops of fat in the milk stick together to form butter.

SALAMANDER

AMPHIBIAN

Frogs, toads, salamanders, and newts are amphibians. The word *amphibian* means "double life" because these animals live part of their lives in water and part of their lives on land. An amphibian starts life in the water and then lives on land as an adult.

Amphibians lay their eggs in the water. These eggs do not have a hard shell. They are more like jelly. Young amphibians that hatch from the eggs look very different from adult amphibians. The young breathe with gills. They have tails that help them swim.

As young amphibians grow, their bodies change. They grow legs. Lungs develop and their gills disappear. These changes allow amphibians to live on land and breathe air with their lungs.

The skin of amphibians is not protected by hair, feathers, or scales like other animals. Their skin is permeable, which means they can absorb air and water through their skin.

Amphibians are found on all the continents except Antarctica. They are ancient animals that have been around for about 360 million years. However, their lives are being seriously threatened in today's world.

TREE FROG
Most amphibian species are frogs. This is a common tree frog.

ALERT!

Scientists know of approximately 6,000 different kinds of amphibians, but this number could change quickly. Scientists say that more than 120 amphibian species have already disappeared from the world. These kinds of amphibians are extinct, meaning that all members of the species have died.

Many different things are threatening the lives of amphibians, including habitat loss, pollution, introduced species, and a parasitic fungus. Scientists say that 2,000 to 3,000 of the amphibian species in the world are now threatened with extinction. It is the biggest extinction crisis in today's world.

NEWT
Most newts and salamanders are found in the cool forests of North America, Europe, and northern Asia.

This fire salamander lives in Hungary.

Habitat Loss and Pollution

Amphibians often live in swamps and ponds. But many of these swamps and ponds are being filled in to make way for roads, houses, and malls. Amphibians also live in rain forests that are being cut down or destroyed by fire. The loss of these habitats often leaves the amphibians nowhere to live.

Clean water is extremely important to amphibians. Adult amphibians need clean water to keep their skin moist. Adults lay their eggs in water, and young amphibians live completely in water.

Some ponds and creeks are close to farms. Chemical fertilizers are used on farms to grow better crops.

Pesticides are used to kill insects that destroy crops. However, when it rains, these chemicals are washed into the nearby ponds and creeks that lead to swamps and rivers.

Many frogs in these areas have been found with deformities, such as missing legs or extra legs. Deformed frogs like these have been found in 44 of the 50 United States. Some scientists believe that the chemical pollution in the water is absorbed by the soft eggs of amphibians and by their permeable skin. The chemical pollution affects the eggs and growth of the young, causing these deformities.

Blue poison dart frogs are endangered and found only in five forests of Suriname in South America.

Introduced Species and Fungus

Since the 1930s African clawed frogs have been shipped around the world by the thousands. These frogs are used in laboratory studies and for other purposes. Some exotic amphibians are shipped to other countries as pets or for food. Sometimes these amphibians escape or are released into their new habitat. In their new habitat they can cause problems.

The introduction of African clawed frogs into new areas has caused two major problems. African clawed frogs are more aggressive than many frogs, and they have been known to eat other frogs. But the bigger problem is that African clawed frogs carry a fungus called amphibian chytrid (KIT rid). This fungus does not hurt African clawed frogs, but it is deadly to many other kinds of amphibians.

This cane toad lives in the Amazon jungle in Peru.

Scientists discovered this fungus in 1993. In the wild the fungus is unstoppable and untreatable. It can kill 80 percent of the amphibians in an area within months. Scientists suspect that dozens of frog species have gone extinct because of this fungus.

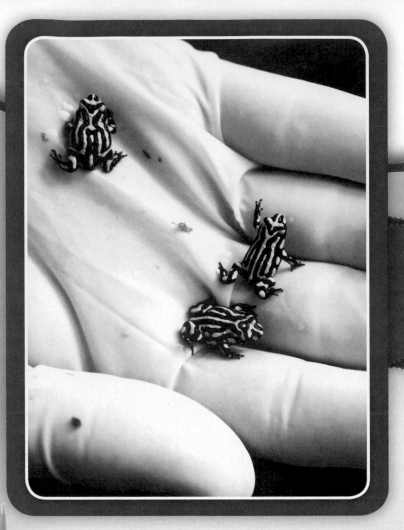

About 130 critically endangered Corroboree frogs are being protected and preserved at Taronga Zoo in Sydney, Australia. Only about 200 of these frogs are left in the wild.

Plans to Help

Scientists and conservation groups from around the world are putting plans together to help save amphibians. Much of their work focuses on the amphibian chytrid fungus because the disease it causes is the most serious and immediate threat.

Some scientists are researching how the disease spreads and why it kills only some individuals in one species, but kills all of another species. Other scientists are assessing the damage the disease has caused. The areas most affected so far include Central America, the Caribbean, Australia, and parts of Asia. However, scientists warn there is no continent or amphibian species that is safe.

Conservation groups that include many zoos are taking in many of the threatened amphibian species to protect and preserve them. In the future when the research scientists find ways to control the disease, the conservation groups will release these animals back into their natural habitat.

What We Can Do

Like scientists, you can do research and learn as much as you can about the problems facing frogs and other amphibians. You can search the Internet using search words, such as *threats to frogs and amphibians*, for more information. You can find maps and lists of the amphibian species in your area.

Amphibians live all over North America and in every state of the United States. The Appalachian range is home to many different species. Contact local nature preserves, zoos, or the office of environmental matters in your state to learn about volunteer opportunities.

You can also help by keeping local ponds and creeks clean. Although these small habitats may not seem as important as others, they are home to many creatures. We need to help preserve a future for them as well as for us.

A zookeeper at Taronga Zoo cares for Corroboree frog eggs (photo at right), tadpoles, and young frogs. Zoos all around the world are developing similar conservation programs to protect amphibian species from extinction.

Toad by the Road

by Joanne Ryder

I'm only a toad
By the side of the road,
Watching the world go by.
Some hustle and hurry.
Some bustle and scurry.
Some wiggle, flicker, or fly.
They come and they go
On their way to and fro.
But I'd rather sit and sing.
It's a glorious day,
So I'm happy to stay
And savor the songs of spring.

THE POISON-DART FROGS

by Douglas Florian

Brown with oval orange spots.
Crimson mottled black with blots.
Neon green with blue-black bands.
Tangerine with lemon strands.
Banana yellow.
Ultramarine.
Almost any color seen.
And though their poison can tip a dart,
These frogs are Masters of Fine Art.

Match the MORAL

Three short frog fables follow, but the moral for each has gotten separated from its story. Match the moral to the fable it fits.

Morals

- Look before you leap.
- Choose your friends wisely.
- Beauty is in the eye of the beholder.

The Frogs and the Well

Two frogs lived in a small pond, but one hot summer it dried up. While looking for a new home, they came to a deep well.

"This looks like a cool, wet place to live. Let's dive in," said one frog.

"Not so fast, my friend. What if this well dries up like the pond? How would we get out?" replied the other frog.

Frog and Toad

A frog and a toad were sitting by a pond. Each thought himself handsome and the other ugly. A girl passed by and saw the two. "Yuck!" she cried as she ran away, disgusted by both.

The Mouse, the Frog, and the Hawk

A mouse and a frog were friends. One day the frog thought it would be fun to tie his leg to the mouse's. This was fine while they were in the meadow. Later, though, the frog hopped to the pond with the mouse. The poor mouse couldn't swim and drowned. A passing hawk snatched them both and flew to its nest. Still tied to the mouse, the frog also became the hawk's dinner.

Word Relationships

An *analogy* is a comparison of two sets of words. Each set of words has a similar relationship. Sometimes the words are *synonyms*, with similar meanings. Sometimes they are *antonyms,* with opposite meanings. The words in the example analogy have opposite meanings.

Example: *good* is to *bad* as *clean* is to *polluted*

Use the words in the box to complete the analogies.

ancient	extinct	habitat	major	preserve

1 alive is to _____ as right is to wrong

2 quard is to protect as save is to _____

3 home is to neighborhood as pond is to _____

4 old is to _____ as new is to current

5 _____ is to minor as large is to little

Hint:

Think about the relationship of the words to help you pick the right answer.

31

SAVE the FROGS!

and other amphibians

In "Amphibian Alert!" you learned about some of the problems that amphibians are facing in the world today. Create a board game about amphibians that are losing their home for one of the reasons given in the article. Have the amphibians look for a new home.

After you have drawn up the plan for your board game, write a set of instructions for how to play the game.

START

Pond is too small.

Lose one turn.

Frog finds safe home with clean water!

FINISH

- Start with a sentence that states what the instructions are for.
- List all necessary materials.
- List each step in the game. Make sure the steps are in the right order.
- Tell how the game is won.

Remember to write each step in your instructions as a complete sentence.

Pond is polluted by chemicals.

Go back 3 spaces.

Deadly fungus in the area.

Return to start.

African clawed frogs live here.

Go back 2 spaces.

33

Museums
Worlds of Wonder

Museums are wonderful places.

That doesn't just mean "terrific places." It means places that fill you with wonder—that surprise and amaze you. It also means places that *make* you wonder—about the world, about nature, about history, about people.

How do museums do that? No two museums do it in the same way. There are art museums, science museums, historical museums, and nature museums. There are museums that focus on a single subject, like music boxes or postage stamps, and there are museums that seem to go in dozens of different directions at once.

Here is a brief tour of five museums that are very different from each other. But all of them are full of wonders.

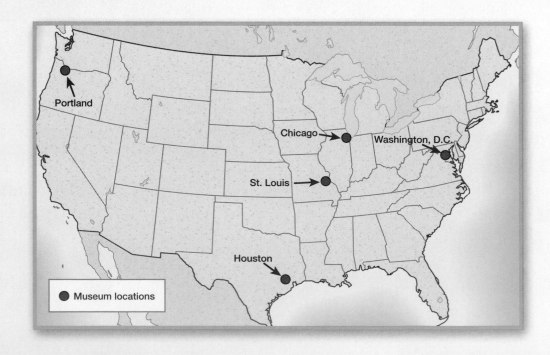

Portland

Chicago →

Washington, D.C.

St. Louis →

Houston →

● Museum locations

City Museum of St. Louis, Missouri

The first thing you should know about the City Museum of St. Louis is that it is located in an old shoe factory. It's no surprise, then, that this museum believes in preserving the past and recycling—making something new out of something old. There's also an amazing playground called MonstroCity that's made mostly of recycled materials from the city of St. Louis, including giant metal springs, a castle turret, and the body of a jet plane.

Artist Bob Cassilly designed the City Museum as a huge work of art. Take the Enchanted Caves. Where shoes once moved on conveyor belts through tunnels, children now run into petrified dragons and climb spiral staircases. In Art City, you can watch glass blowers at work, and make your own work of art, too. Then there's the museum *inside* the museum. It's called The Museum of Mirth, Mystery, and Mayhem and it's like an old-fashioned carnival. Finally, let's not forget the World Aquarium, home to more than 10,000 sea creatures, from stingrays to seahorses.

Are you interested in space and flight? Have you ever wondered where the Wright Brothers' original airplane is? If so, then the National Air and Space Museum is the place for you. It has the largest collection of aircraft and spacecraft in the world.

Begin with the Milestones of Flight Exhibit. You'll see the *Spirit of St. Louis*, the first plane to be flown nonstop across the Atlantic Ocean by a solo pilot. Want some faster fliers? Check out the *Airacomet*, the first American jet, and the X-15, which flew six times the speed of sound! Upstairs you'll find the airplane that made it all possible: the *Flyer*, which Orville and Wilbur Wright first flew in 1903.

Next, let your imagination soar into space. This museum is home to *Sputnik I*, the first satellite to successfully orbit Earth, and the *Apollo 11* command module, which carried the first men to the moon. Here also are replicas of spacecraft that have flown to Mars, Venus, and Jupiter.

The Albert Einstein Planetarium lets you feel what it might be like to zoom through the galaxy. The Ride Simulator takes you on a virtual space walk. Finally, there is a real moon rock you can touch that the *Apollo 17* astronauts brought back.

Field Museum
in Chicago, Illinois

You could spend days exploring the Field Museum in the city of Chicago. The museum contains more than twenty million items, including mummies, meteorites, and mammals. With so much to see, you might not have time to meet Sue. That would be a mistake.

Sue is the largest *Tyrannosaurus rex* skeleton ever found, as well as the most complete. Sue is forty-two feet long with more than two hundred bones—real bones, not plaster ones. All except for Sue's second skull. It's a case of two heads being better than one.

Sue's five-foot-long skull was so big and heavy that the museum staff had to put it in a glass case by itself. They made a lighter model for the skeleton on display. You can put your nose just inches from Sue's real skull—if you dare. You also can handle models of some of Sue's bones, including a huge tooth and a rib. By the way, Sue was named after Sue Hendrickson, the woman who found "her" in South Dakota. No one really knows if Sue is male or female.

World Forestry Center and Discovery Museum
in Portland, Oregon

A museum that's about trees? The World Forestry Center's Discovery Museum will make you appreciate forests more than ever before—including forests around the world.

On the first floor of the museum, you can explore forests that grow in the Pacific Northwest. You can discover what lives under the forest and then take a ride to explore the tree-tops. On another ride you can learn how smokejumpers fight forest fires. The museum shows the many things that forests provide, such as wood, water, habitat, and clean air.

On the second floor, a giant wall map tells about different types of forests worldwide. Then you can see for yourself. Take a train ride to the forests of Siberia and a boat ride to a forest lake in China. Ride a jeep to visit forest animals in South Africa. Look down on the canopy of Brazil's Amazon rainforest.

American Cowboy Museum
at Taylor-Stevenson Ranch
near Houston, Texas

Many museums are important for changing old ideas people may have. Through hands-on exhibits, talks, and even horseback riding, the American Cowboy Museum gives the true history of a popular legend. There is a lot we can learn about the American cowboy. For example, did you know that as many as one-third of all cowboys were African Americans? Many cowboys were Native Americans, and the first cowboys, or *vaqueros*, were from Mexico. And of course, "cowboys" also included women.

The museum is part of the Taylor-Stevenson Ranch, which is 150 years old. It has been owned by generations of an African American family. About fifty years ago, the family started the museum to honor the part Native Americans, African Americans, Hispanics, and women played in settling the West. The founders, Mollie Stevenson, Jr. and her mother, Mollie Stevenson, Sr. are also the first living African Americans in the National Cowgirl Hall of Fame.

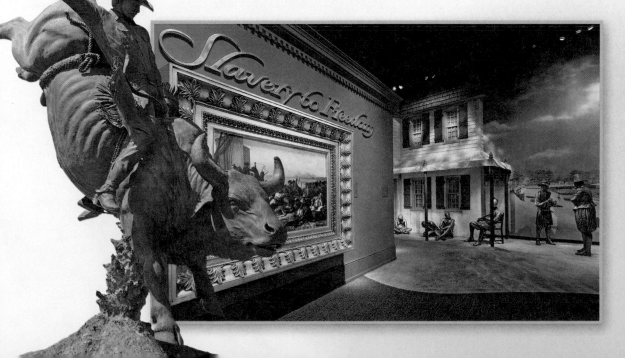

MAKING THE MOST FROM
TRASH

Trash is a huge problem. We make mountains of it every day. But there are three things we can do to help fix the problem. First, we can REDUCE what we use. Second, we can REUSE things, rather than just throw them away. Third, we can RECYCLE. Often one thing can be recycled into something entirely different.

Flakes to Fleece

Did you know that plastic bottles can have a second life as a fleece jacket? Here's how. The plastic bottles are cleaned and chopped into flakes. Later, the flakes are melted down and squeezed into threads. Like wool, the threads are spun into yarn and woven into fleece. The fleece can be sewn into a jacket, hat, or a warm pair of socks. It takes about twenty-five two-liter plastic soda bottles to make a jacket.

Tires to Playgrounds

Where do all the old tires go? The lucky ones are recycled into firm but bouncy playground surfaces. Maybe you have felt how comfortable it is to walk in a rubber-soled shoe. Well, someone had the idea to chop up old tires and mold the rubber pieces into a squishy rubber surface for playgrounds. It saves children from being hurt, it recycles rubber, and it's fun to play on! So go ahead and bounce!

Milk Jugs to Chairs

Have you ever noticed the number two inside a triangle on the bottom of a milk jug? That symbol means the milk jug could have another life as a chair. Type two plastic, also called HDPE, gets recycled into all kinds of sturdy furniture. It looks like painted wood, but it will last longer. You can even buy trash cans made from recycled plastic. How fitting is that?

Dinosaur Bone

by Alice Schertle

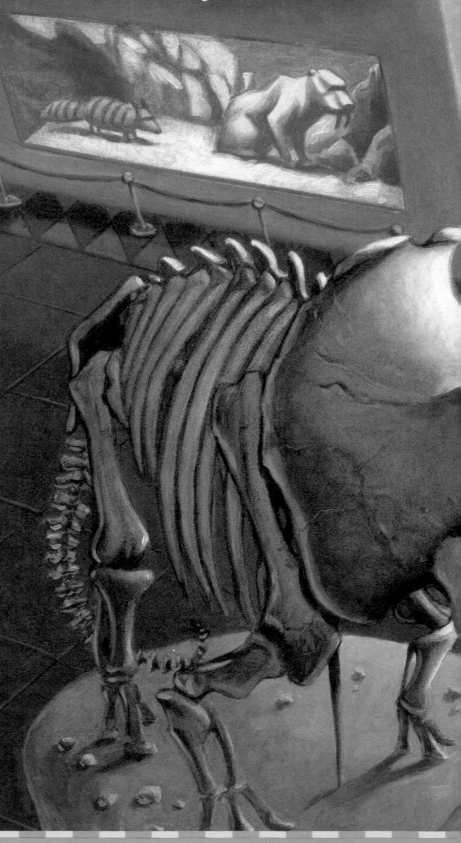

Dinosaur bone
alone, alone;
keeping a secret
old as stone

deep in the mud
asleep in the mud
tell me, tell me,
dinosaur bone

What was the world
when the seas were new
and ferns unfurled
and strange winds blew?

Were the mountains fire?
Were the rivers ice?
Was it mud and mire?
Was it paradise?

How did it smell,
your earth, your sky?
How did you live?
How did you die?

How long have you lain
alone, alone?
Tell me, tell me,
dinosaur bone.

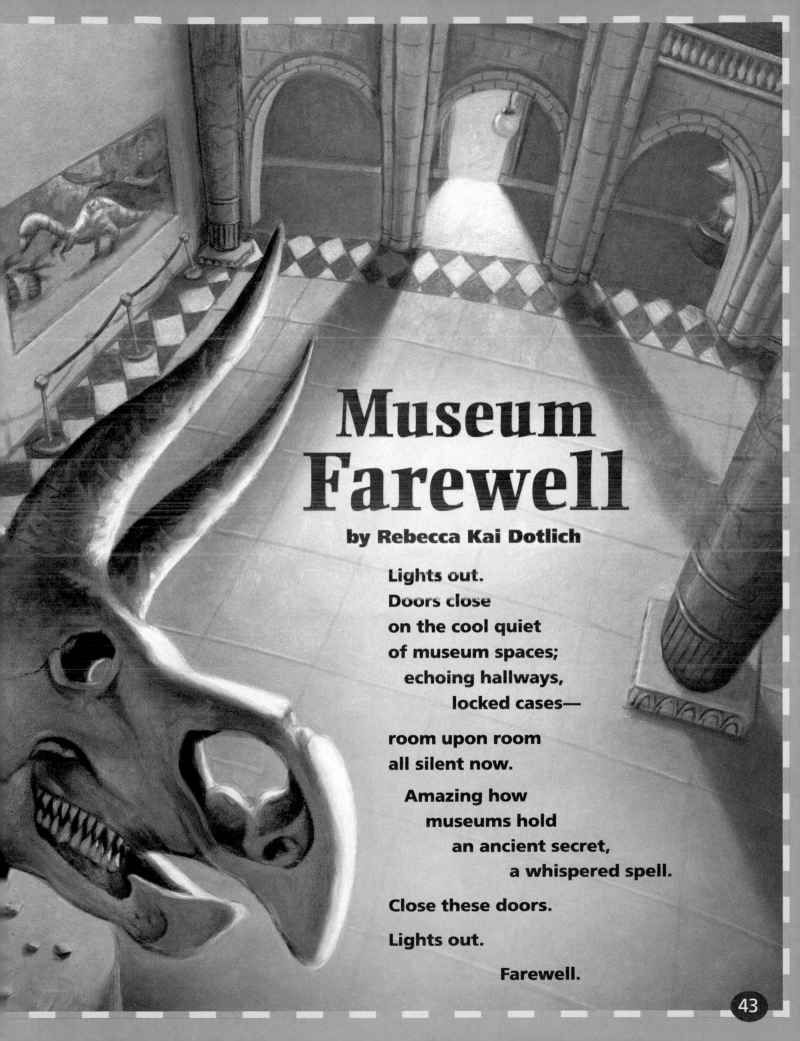

Museum Farewell

by Rebecca Kai Dotlich

Lights out.
Doors close
on the cool quiet
of museum spaces;
echoing hallways,
locked cases—

room upon room
all silent now.

Amazing how
museums hold
an ancient secret,
a whispered spell.

Close these doors.

Lights out.

Farewell.

Activity Central

Come to the MUSEUM!

Museums often advertise to tell people about new or special exhibits. Create an ad for a real or imaginary museum. You might design your ad as a jingle to sing on the radio, a billboard, or a poster. Include in your ad three facts about the museum a visitor would need to know. Your ad might tell where the museum is located, when it's open, and what its special exhibits are. You could also include quotes from people who have visited the museum. For example, "Ed Crowe" might say: "I think this is the best museum I've ever been to!"

Meet Sue, the largest and most complete T-rex skeleton ever found!

"It's thrilling!" exclaims Lisa

"Awesome" Joe agrees

Sue is 42 feet long with more than 200 real bones. Sue resides at the Field Museum in Chicago.

Impossible? NOT!

The poem below is about exploring with words. However, some of its words are missing! The words in the box have the prefixes *im-* and *in-*. On another sheet of paper, use each word to fill in the blanks. Check the spelling of the prefix and base word that make up each word.

inexpensive	injustice	independence
incredible	immeasurable	

Climb to the top of Mount Everest
And take in the _____ view.
Explore the sea's _____ depths
With Captain Nemo and his daring crew.

March with Martin Luther King Jr.
to protest _____ in our nation.
Listen to Thomas Jefferson speak
Of _____ and unfair taxation.

Impossible! Improbable! Is that what you say?
Well, that's incorrect! You can do it today.

Exploring can be _____.
It doesn't have to cost you a dime.
All you need are two simple things:
An interesting book and some time!

Your Turn

EXPRESS YOURSELF!

Is your school or community doing what it can to recycle its trash? Do you see ways that recycling could be improved? Express your opinion, or yours and a partner's, in a letter to a leader of your school or community.

Tell what's working or, if necessary, include your own ideas to improve recycling efforts. For example, maybe each classroom could have a bin for recycling paper. Coming up with suggestions helps support your opinion.

WRITING TIPS

- Begin your letter by giving an example of the problem.

- State your opinion of the situation.

- Be positive about how the problem could be handled.

- Suggest possible solutions and offer to help.

Save Timber Woods!

Cast of Characters
**Narrator • Lucas • Laura
Gina • Hector**

Scene I

Setting: The kitchen in Gina's home on the edge of the woods

Narrator: Laura, Gina, Hector, and Lucas are researching a current event for school. Gina is searching on a laptop. The others are looking through newspapers.

Lucas: What if we do our report on gas prices?

Laura: Boring!

(Suddenly, Gina sees a deer outside in the yard. She jumps up from her chair and dashes to the kitchen door, shouting.)

Gina: Get out of there! Scram!

(Grabbing a broom, Gina charges out the door, waving the broom and yelling as the deer runs away.)

Laura: Why did you yell at that deer, Gina? It was so cute.

Gina *(Outraged)*: Cute? Maybe, if you only see them once in a while; but they've started to show up in our yard every day. They are eating the tree we planted when my little sister was born!

Narrator: Gina points at a small tree on the lawn. Its branches are nearly bare.

Gina *(Calming down)*: Those deer and our neighborhood don't go together.

Hector: We have deer at my house, too. My dad says it's because the deer have no place to go. People are building homes where the deer used to live. Now they have to find food somewhere else.

Gina *(In an annoyed voice)*: Well, not in my backyard.

Lucas: The poor deer lost their homes, Gina.

Gina: Well, my poor family is losing our favorite tree.

Hector *(Holding up the newspaper he's been looking through, excitedly)*: Hey! Listen to this! Here's an article that says the deer problem is going to get worse. Land developers plan to cut down Timber Woods, by the school. Our town government has been renting the woods from a private owner. Now the owner plans to sell it to a developer who plans to build one hundred townhouses.

Laura: Timber Woods? That's where we do fieldwork for science class. That's where we camp and have picnics.

Lucas: What about the animals who live there? More animals will get kicked out of their homes.

Gina: More yards will be ruined by deer!

Hector: Well, at least we found a current event to report on.

Laura: I wish we could stop them from cutting down Timber Woods.

Hector: Maybe it's not too late. The paper says that people can talk about the development plan at next week's town council meeting. Let's ask our parents if we can go. Right now, let's find more information to put into our current events report.

Gina: Let's get all the facts. That way we'll have a good report for class and good ideas for the council meeting.

Lucas: Maybe our friends will come to the meeting.

Narrator: The group presents its current events report and the whole class gets excited. The class decides to ask the town's leaders to buy Timber Woods and preserve the land for both animals and people.

Scene II

Setting: The next day, in the dining room of Gina's home

Narrator: The four friends are making signs for the meeting. Gina and Lucas are working on a large sign.

Laura: What is your sign going to say?

Gina and Lucas: "Save Timber Woods."

Lucas: "Save the animals from us . . . "

Gina: ". . . and save our yards from the animals!"

Hector: It's about the woods, too. Remember that book we read about the water cycle? It said that natural areas, such as woods, help absorb water and prevent flooding when heavy rains fall or snow melts. But how can I put that on a sign?

Laura: How about: "Woods and water—important partners. Ask me why."

Hector: Good idea! Then I can talk about it when I give our statement.

Gina: It's cool that the town council said you could present a statement from us, Hector. But how will the town ever get enough money to buy the woods? I also heard my mom talking about how much money the city will get from new taxpayers who move into the new houses.

Lucas: But the problems caused by cutting the woods will cost money. We have to help them see that.

Hector *(Pointing at Lucas)*: You're right. Instead of ignoring the issue of money, we should show that we understand it. Let's do some more research so we know the facts. And how about this for a sign: "Saving Timber Woods saves dollars and makes sense."

Laura: At least the town will know how we feel.

Scene III

Setting: A meeting room with rows of folding chairs, inside the town hall

Hector: I'm nervous.

Laura: You're going to be great, Hector. Look, I think that's the developer!

Hector: Maybe he could tear down those old Smithfield warehouses and build homes there. Nobody has used those buildings for a long time.

Lucas: Good idea. *(Turning around)* I think the meeting's about to start.

Narrator: The town council members soon introduce the main topic: the sale of Timber Woods. People take turns talking about the plan to build townhouses. Finally, it's Hector's turn to speak. The audience listens closely as he explains why the woods are so important, and what the students want the council to do.

Hector *(In a firm voice)*: So, we ask the adults in town to join us in finding a way to turn Timber Woods into protected parkland.

(He sits down as many people applaud.)

Narrator: After more debate, the council decides to delay the sale of Timber Woods for three months. During that time, the town will try to raise enough money to buy the woods. After the meeting, the students get together.

Gina *(In an excited voice)*: They listened to us after all.

Laura: Now we have to help find ways to raise money.

Lucas: How about a bake sale?

Hector: That's a good idea, but we'll need to do more than that.

Laura: Let's meet tomorrow.

Gina: Let's involve the whole class. Everyone will benefit if we can save Timber Woods, so we should all work together.

Reading the Play
With a partner, describe the structural features of the play—the scenes, dialogue, and stage directions—and discuss how they helped you follow the events.

FOLLOWING MUIR:

A Persuasive Essay

John Muir was a protector of nature. He set an example that each of us can follow to protect the natural areas around us.

The first way we can follow Muir's example is to discover our local natural areas. Muir was a great walker. He once walked one thousand miles from Indiana to Florida. He also took a 250-mile walk from San Francisco, California, to the Yosemite (yoh SEH mih tee) Valley, in the heart of the Sierra Nevada Mountains.

Another way to follow Muir is to learn about nature. Muir loved to explore the outdoors. He learned everything he could about rocks, plants, and animals. From his exploring, he came to realize that the wilderness, places where people do not live or build, is an important gift. Muir decided that his life's goal was to protect this gift.

Muir's greatest example for us is his work to protect nature. He shared its beauty by writing books. He climbed Yosemite's towering peaks and described them as "clothed in light." In winter, he delighted in its "pearl-gray belt of snow." However, he also saw sheep eating Yosemite's plants and people chopping down its trees for wood. Muir gave talks and wrote books about these dangers. President Theodore Roosevelt was so impressed after hearing Muir that he visited Yosemite. In 1890, Roosevelt signed a bill making Yosemite a national park. This meant that the U.S. government would take care of it.

We can find our own pieces of nature to explore, learn about, and protect. We can write to our local newspapers about nature's beauty and tell people how to help care for it. We can all follow in John Muir's footsteps.

John Muir Timeline

1838	Born in Scotland
1849	Family moves to the United States
1867	Walks from Indiana to Florida
1868	Walks from San Francisco to Yosemite Valley
1890	Helps Yosemite become a national park
1892	Forms the Sierra Club
1903	Camps with President Theodore Roosevelt in Yosemite
1912	Travels to South America and Africa
1914	Dies of pneumonia on December 24

Analyzing the Essay

On a sheet of paper, list details the author used that you think helped persuade the reader. Explain to a partner why you think so.

The Comb of Trees
A Secret Sign Along the Way

By Claudia Lewis

Riding to Rock Creek
for our picnics
we swing around
a certain curve
and then I see it—

Standing high
on a mountain ridge
a little row
of firs, with trunks
tall and bare,
lined up one by one—
a comb
against the sky.

As we draw near
each time
I wonder—

it…?
  Is it…?

    Then we turn—

    Yes! It's there!

No storm
has wrecked my comb,
no lumberjack
has chopped it down—

All's well
still
(a while?)
up there.

Enjoy the Earth

Yoruba, Africa

Enjoy the earth gently
Enjoy the earth gently
For if the earth is spoiled
It cannot be repaired
Enjoy the earth gently

The Impact of Life's Events

Your timeline should end with an arrow to show that the line will continue.

1st

Spelling Bee

A timeline of a person's life often includes events that impact or shape the person. Look back at the essay about John Muir. The timeline shows important events that shaped who he was. It also shows the dates for when he was born and when he died.

Create a timeline about your life. Include the year of your birth and four important events in your life.

Write About It Choose one event from your timeline. Write a paragraph telling about the event and why it was important.

Born

Your timeline begins with a point and gives the date you were born.

Say It with a Sign

Tear down warehouses— NOT WOODS!

Preserve our Picnic Place!

People use signs to show their feelings in a public place, as the students do in "Save Timber Woods!" The students want the town council to know how they feel about the proposed sale of Timber Woods to a developer. So they make signs that the people going to the meeting will see.

Make a sign that the students in the story could use to save Timber Woods. Or make a sign about a local habitat you want to save. Try to make your message clear in as few words as possible.

Try to See

In "Save Timber Woods!" the friends persuade a town to protect a threatened woodland habitat. The photos on these pages show four common woodland animals. Choose one, or a different animal whose habitat might be in danger. Write a persuasive essay explaining why it is important to protect the animal's home. Use "Following Muir: A Persuasive Essay" as a model for writing your essay.

Be sure to include the following:
- an introductory paragraph that states the point you will be making
- at least three reasons or examples that support that point
- one paragraph for each reason or example
- a concluding paragraph that restates the point you have made

It My Way!

MYSTERY

Once a week, Ms. Cabrera's science class spent an afternoon outside, working in teams to observe different habitats. Adrian, Mara, and Nicole were assigned pond patrol. Adrian wondered if his team had gotten the best assignment because of his extra-sharp eyes.

Reed's Pond lay at the end of a shady, sloping path. Pine trees towered overhead. Bushes and moss-covered rocks rimmed the shore. Adrian had been the first one in class to spot the turtle at the pond—even though its brown shell and wrinkled skin blended in perfectly with its surroundings.

"Here, Brownie . . . here, Brownie," Adrian whispered as he approached the water's edge. But today, the turtle that peeked from the water looked different. Instead of a little brown face, this one

had streaks of red near each eye.

"Brownie? Are you wearing makeup?" From what Adrian could see, the turtle's shell looked different, too. Today it was green with yellow stripes.

at Reed's Pond

The girls hurried over. When the turtle came up for another breath, Nicole noticed the changes, too.

"That's not Brownie. That's a different kind of turtle," she said. "Its name should be Red Dot."

"Maybe Brownie's somewhere else," said Mara.

They continued their pond patrol, but Adrian had a strange feeling that something wasn't right. Sure enough, his hunch was correct.

"Look!" Mara shouted. She was pointing at a bird's nest or what used to be a bird's nest.

Just last week they had written about the nest in their logs. It was a carefully made cup of sticks nestled in a low-hanging branch. There had been three brown eggs in it. Now the branch was broken. The bowl was squashed into a messy ball.

"Where are the eggs?" asked Nicole.

Adrian crouched under the branch, which jutted out over some rocks at the water's edge. He saw one egg smashed into a crevice between two rocks. He couldn't see any sign of the other two eggs.

"Do you think an animal did this to the nest?" Nicole wondered.

"An animal couldn't have turned Brownie into Red Dot," said Adrian.

"And an animal wouldn't have left this," said Mara. She held up a shopping bag that she had found. "There's lettuce in it. Maybe it's a clue."

"A clue to what?" asked Nicole.

Ms. Cabrera's whistle blew. It was time to go back to class.

"We need to do some more investigating," said Mara. "Let's meet here Saturday, when we have more time."

The weather on Saturday was sunny and warm, but no one else was at the pond. Nicole, Mara, and Adrian scanned the area. Adrian soon found the new turtle. It sat basking on a rock at the edge of the water. When it saw the three children, it quickly slid into the water. The ripples spread and soon faded. Then Adrian, Mara, and Nicole went to investigate the bird's nest. The clump of sticks remained, but there were no new clues about what had destroyed the nest or where the two eggs had gone.

Many turtles like to bask, or warm themselves, in the sun.

"This is the case of the missing turtle and eggs," Mara said.

"Shh," whispered Adrian. He could hear leaves crunching on the path. "Someone's coming. Hide!"

The three crouched in the bushes. Through the leaves, they could see a teenaged boy wearing a blue backpack. At the edge of the pond, the boy swung it from his shoulder and knelt down. Adrian held his breath. He could hear his heart beating. Had the boy noticed them?

The boy seemed to think he was alone, however. He reached into his backpack and pulled out a turtle whose shell was as big as a plate. It was bright green, with yellow and green markings on the belly. Suddenly the turtle's head shot out of the shell and snapped at the boy's wrist. The boy dropped the turtle into the pond. The splash rang out as loud as a slap. Adrian saw the red dashes on the turtle's face.

The boy darted back up the path and quickly vanished.

"So that's where Red Dot came from," whispered Nicole.

"Red Dot was already here on Thursday, though," said Adrian. "This is the same kind of turtle, but it's not the *same* turtle. Also, what about Brownie? Where's he?"

"We've got to talk to that boy," said Mara. "Come on." Adrian wasn't sure it was a good idea, but Mara was already running up the path. He and Nicole followed.

"Excuse me!" Mara called out when she reached the field. The boy turned to look but kept striding toward his bike.

"I just want to ask you about the turtle," Mara said.

"I don't know what you're talking about," the boy said. "I don't know anything about turtles." He got on his bike.

"We just saw you drop one into the pond!" Mara shouted. It didn't matter. The boy pedaled off without looking back.

"Something fishy is going on," Nicole said.

"Something turtle-y, you mean," replied Adrian.

"I think it's time for a little research," said Mara.

Red-eared sliders are popular pets.

On Monday, they told Ms. Cabrera what they had seen. During science, she gave them time to research on the computer. Mara typed the words *red dot turtle* into the search engine. Links for turtleneck sweaters, Turtle Island, and a video game came up.

"This won't help," said Nicole.

"Don't give up yet," said Mara. She typed in *red turtle*. That was better. Lots of listings appeared for a turtle called a red-eared slider. The first thing Mara did was to click on the images.

"That's it!" said Adrian, as a photo appeared. "That's Red Dot, all right."

With a few more mouse-clicks, the students learned that the turtles were common pets. They also learned that the red-eared slider's natural habitat was east of the Rocky Mountains. "So what is one doing in a pond in California?" asked Nicole.

Mara typed *red-eared slider in California* into the search engine.

Among the listings of turtles for sale and questions about pet turtles, they saw an article from a California paper. The three of them read silently.

The article told about people dumping their pet turtles into local waters and the problems that occurred as a result. "Mystery solved!" said Mara.

"Ms. Cabrera!" they called.

"It looks like the pond patrol might have uncovered some illegal activity," Ms. Cabrera said when they told her what they had learned. "Let's report it to the water district."

That Thursday, Ms. Cabrera's class had a special observation day at the pond. Mr. Roberts, an officer from the water district, was with them. He had brought nets for capturing the red-eared sliders. Adrian spotted the first one, basking near the ruined bird's nest. Working together, the class helped Mr. Roberts catch two more.

"We'll take them to a turtle sanctuary," Mr. Roberts explained. "It's a place where they keep the turtles safe until someone can adopt them."

While Mr. Roberts talked, Adrian was looking for his old friend.

"Brownie!" said Adrian when he saw the head peek up. "Look, Mr. Roberts. That's the turtle I'm used to seeing."

"That's a western pond turtle. It's just the kind of turtle we want to see around here."

"I never knew what kind he was. I just knew I liked him," said Adrian. *Western pond turtle*, he wrote in his log.

Western pond turtles live in California, Oregon, and Washington.

"We got the sliders out just in time. Red-eared sliders are big. They eat the same things as the western pond turtles, and the western pond turtles can't compete," said Mr. Roberts.

"What about the bird eggs?" asked Nicole. "Did the turtles have anything to do with those?"

"Probably, but we can't be sure," said Mr. Roberts. "Red-eared sliders like to bask on nests. They can squash the nests and crush the eggs."

"That's another reason why people shouldn't leave their pets here," said Ms. Cabrera. She was posting a sign on a tree. DON'T DUMP YOUR PETS. BRING PET TURTLES TO VALLEY TURTLE SANCTUARY.

"Thanks for helping us save the native species," Mr. Roberts told the class. "I have something for Adrian, Mara, and Nicole." He handed them each an envelope and a patch that said *Water District* with a picture of a river.

"The water district invites you to be its first junior officers," Mr. Roberts said. "We'd also like to offer each of you a scholarship to ecology camp this summer. You can talk it over with your parents."

"Thanks!" said Adrian. He'd never thought his sharp eyes would actually help wildlife survive.

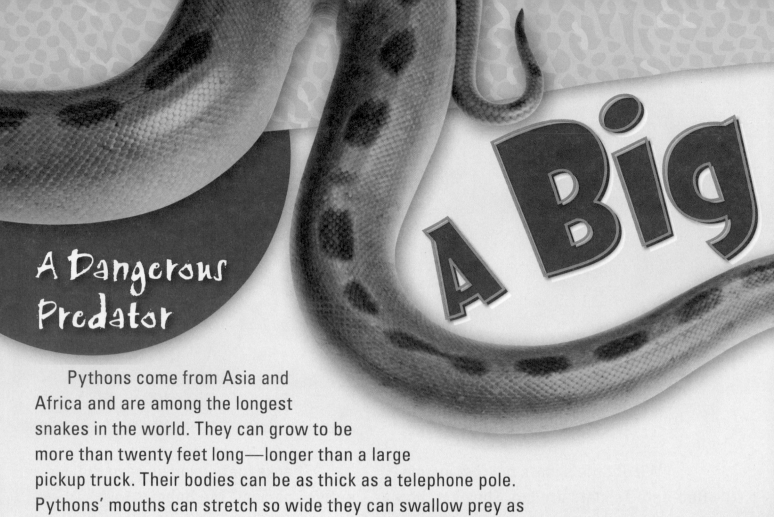

A Big

A Dangerous Predator

Pythons come from Asia and Africa and are among the longest snakes in the world. They can grow to be more than twenty feet long—longer than a large pickup truck. Their bodies can be as thick as a telephone pole. Pythons' mouths can stretch so wide they can swallow prey as large as deer and alligators.

Surprisingly, baby pythons are popular pets in this country. But pythons grow quickly. In a year, a tiny baby can become an eight-foot long snake. As time passes, it grows even bigger. Many owners have trouble caring for such large, dangerous animals. Sometimes, they take their snake and leave it in the wild.

In most areas of the United States, pythons wouldn't have enough warmth, water, or space to survive. Places like southern Florida, though, have a perfect climate for pythons. Because of this, pythons are causing serious trouble in Florida's Everglades National Park.

Adult pythons can weigh up to 200 pounds.

Python Problem

Can the Problem Be Solved?

Scientists are not sure how many pythons are in the Everglades, but they estimate that there are thousands. The big snakes eat the animals that make their natural home in the park. Some of these animals are endangered, such as the Key Largo cotton mouse and the white ibis, a water bird. Pythons have also eaten the pets of people who live in the area.

Park officials are trying to solve this big problem. They are using different methods to capture pythons. They have tried using radio transmitters to lure snakes to places where they can be caught. And they have even trained a dog to help. "Python Pete" is a beagle that can smell pythons and alert humans to their presence.

Python Pete is doing a good job. But people have to learn not to buy exotic pets they cannot take care of. Teaching people to think through their pet-buying decisions is also part of the fight against the python.

Python Pete has been trained to pick up the scent of pythons.

Naming the Turtle

by Patricia Hubbell

Slowpod,
Weightlifter,
Housemover,
Homelover.

Seaflipper,
Rainstopper,
Pond-land-
and-stream-dweller.

Platepacker,
Boneback,
Hardshell
and Softhat.

Clicktoe
and Stare-eye,
Budhead
and Stemneck.

Nob-bob and
Lookslow,
Spotback
and Ridgetop.

Plod-plod
and Plopplop,

Logloving
Rockstone.

Greater Flamingo

by Tony Johnston

Pale as the pink lip
of a shell, it drinks from its
cool green reflection

Activity Central

You Be The Detective

Read about the events below. From the set of clues, draw a conclusion about what happened.

The Missing Clown Fish

The Ringling School's Grade 4 class has a saltwater aquarium. It contains an eel and three large angelfish. On Monday, a family donates two colorful clown fish. On Tuesday morning, Roy Gee, "the class clown," reports one clown fish missing. What happened?

CLUES

- The school's night janitor says the clown fish looked fine at 7:00 p.m.
- Roy Gee says he'll be the other clown fish's friend.
- The three large angelfish are still in the aquarium and look no different.
- The eel does not eat its regular frozen shrimp on Tuesday morning.
- A book about the care of eels is unopened. In fact, it's covered with a layer of dust.

The eel ate the clown fish. Because the class hadn't read the eel book, they didn't realize the danger. Angelfish are big enough to avoid being eaten by the eel.

76

Choose Your Words

Using just the right word can help a reader understand exactly how something looks, sounds, acts, or feels. The following Found Pet announcement is on a bulletin board. You finish it. On a piece of paper, write a list of words and phrases to fill in the blanks. Make sure they describe the pet and other details exactly.

Have you lost a _____ snake?

I found a snake in _____. The snake looks _____. When I try to hold it, the snake _____. I think it is feeling _____. I think it may be a python, because it _____. The only sound it makes is _____. I'm keeping the snake in _____. Hurry!

Found Snake

House For Rent

Yard Sale

24 Oak St.

Pets Need You!

Having a pet can be hard work. Sometimes pet owners can't take care of their pets any longer but don't know what to do with them. You've read about some problems this causes.

Search on the Internet for information about how to care for pets properly. Then write an essay of at least three paragraphs that an animal shelter employee might hand out to someone thinking about caring for a pet.

ANIMAL SHELTER

Do I have time to care for a pet?

Here are some tips:

🐾 Start with an introduction to possible pet owners. Encourage them to think about whether owning a pet is right for them. End the essay with a conclusion that sums up your ideas.

🐾 Give examples of the responsibilities of pet ownership (food, water, shelter, exercise).

🐾 Give examples of problems that can be caused when people abandon their pets (problems for the pet, for the environment, and for animal shelters).

🐾 Use a variety of sentence types and clear transitions between paragraphs.

Credits